COLLECTORS' PAPERWEIGHTS

COLLECTORS' PAPERWEIGHTS

PRICE GUIDE AND CATALOGUE

PAPERWEIGHT • PRESS
SANTA CRUZ • CALIFORNIA

L.H. SELMAN LTD.

PAPERWEIGHT SPECIALISTS
761 CHESTNUT STREET
SANTA CRUZ • CALIFORNIA • 95060
TELEPHONE • 408-427-1177 • 800-538-0766

© 1983 by L. H. Selman Ltd.
All rights reserved. No part of this book may be reproduced
in any form without permission of the author.
Library of Congress Catalog Card Number: 82-063071
ISBN: 0-933756-04-6

Dear Collector,

Congratulations! You have taken the first important step in learning about paperweights by ordering COLLECTORS' PAPERWEIGHTS: PRICE GUIDE AND CATALOGUE. The following pages present the finest contemporary limited editions as well as classic, museum-quality weights from the 1840s. The alphabetically listed contemporary artists, studios and companies are briefly described to you. Their individual histories, locations, philosophies and unique artistic features are outlined. Antique paperweight listings follow the contemporary entries.

This catalogue also includes some thoughts on the art of paperweight collecting, a selected bibliography of books and periodicals for your library, and suggested accessories to facilitate your collecting. For your benefit, we have also provided a reference list of contemporary Baccarat sulphides and Gridel animal subjects with their issue date. Cristal d'Albret and Saint Louis sulphide subjects are also listed. Finally, a glossary has been provided to help you fully understand paperweight terminology. Purchase conditions, shipping and other service information accompany an order form at the close of this catalogue.

Since the 1850s, paperweights have been collectibles for many reasons. Discovering their exquisite aesthetic appeal has been our motivating factor. Investment value during inflationary times has been the rationale of others. Still others find paperweights, their history and acquisition, an intellectual challenge. Some find paperweights a unique gift selection. Whatever your reasons are for collecting paperweights, we are always available to help you build an outstanding collection. Your letter or phone call regarding aesthetics, identification, investment potential or gift selection will be promptly and enthusiastically answered. With this catalogue, we express our personal dedication to paperweight collecting and hope to encourage your interest in this very special field.

Sincerely,

Lawrence H. Selman

TABLE OF CONTENTS

THE ART OF COLLECTING	x
BOOKS AND ACCESSORIES	2
CONTEMPORARY PAPERWEIGHTS	8
Rick Ayotte	10
Baccarat	14
Ray and Bob Banford	20
D'Albret	25
"J" Glass	29
Charles Kaziun	35
Lundberg Studios	38
Orient & Flume	41
Perthshire Paperweights	43
Saint Louis	50
Paul Stankard	56
Delmo and Debbie Tarsitano	61
Victor Trabucco	67
Francis Whittemore	70
Paul Ysart	72
Lotton	74
Whitefriars	74
ANTIQUE PAPERWEIGHTS	76
American	77
Baccarat	81
Clichy	88
Saint Louis	94
Whitefriars	102
Bacchus	102
Pantin	103
Bohemian	103
Val St. Lambert	103
PAPERWEIGHT RELATED OBJECTS	106
GLOSSARY	112
SULPHIDES: History and Reference Lists	116

THE ART OF PAPERWEIGHT COLLECTING

HISTORY

Many of the techniques used in the creation of glass paperweights have their origins in ancient Egypt, where the millefiori or "thousand flower" technique was first utilized in mosaics, jewelry, and a variety of functional glass objects.

Handed down and improved upon through the ages, this technique reached the height of popularity during the nineteenth century, when French glass factories began encasing millefiori canes, stylized flowers, and other elements in clear crystal. These beautifully designed and finely crafted works were created by the factories to demonstrate their skills and proficiency and to entice prospective customers. It was during this time, 1840-1860, that paperweights became a unique and highly developed art form.

Over the next forty years, the art spread throughout Europe and to America. Around the turn of the century, production of the objects declined, and it was not until the 1950s that the art of paperweight making was revived. Individual artists in the United States and Scotland and glass factories in France, England, and Scotland began producing fine paperweights in the classic French style as well as experimenting with contemporary designs and techniques.

COLLECTING PAPERWEIGHTS

Even during the nineteenth century, when paperweight production was at its height, people found these small and brilliant works of art desirable collectors' items.

Today, paperweights offer the collector countless hours of discovery and enjoyment as well as an excellent investment opportunity. Over the past thirty years, private collectors, museums, and corporations have watched their collections dramatically increase in value as interest in paperweights and glass art has grown.

Paperweights are available in a wide variety of styles and at a range of prices. Collections can be built on contemporary annual editions or select, antique finds. The glass factories of Perthshire and "J" Glass offer exceptional contemporary weights at moderate prices. Also annual, limited editions from Baccarat, Saint Louis, and American studio artists can be selected to develop an exciting contemporary collection. Sulphides by Baccarat, D'Albret and

Saint Louis offer the beauty of paperweight art as well as a unique way to commemorate and appreciate historic events and personalities. An excellent way to begin an antique collection is by acquiring an example from each of the classic manufacturers: Baccarat, Clichy, and Saint Louis. For all collections, no matter what the theme, quality and taste rather than quantity are the key considerations.

DETERMINING AUTHENTICITY

The most reliable way to determine the provenance and authenticity of a weight is to consult an expert. The next best way is to carefully research the weight in question by studying as many reference sources as are available. It is important to do this before purchasing the weight, as there are many high-priced unauthenticated French "originals" on the market.

Collectors can become familiar with the history of paperweights through a number of excellent books available on the subject and by examining weights first-hand in museums, galleries, and private collections. Also, the Paperweight Collectors' Association, a formal organization founded in 1954, publishes an annual bulletin containing articles on rare paperweights, special collections, conferences, artists, and factories.

L.H. SELMAN LTD.

L.H. Selman Ltd. is most willing to assist you in learning more about paperweights. We have been active in the paperweight field since 1968, promoting and offering our clients the best of the contemporary artists and studios, as well as the finest in antique weights. We have also published *Paperweights for Collectors*, the first comprehensive reference book for collectors. Appraisal services are available to all our collectors. We have recently appraised the Arthur Rubloff Collection of 1100 weights, now a permanent exhibit at the Art Institute of Chicago, the Doheny Collection in Camarillo, California, and the Fowler Collection in Los Angeles. We offer a complete selection of quality antique and contemporary paperweights, backed with years of experience and education in the field, with individuals, corporations and museums numbering among our satisfied clients. We look forward to helping you, too, build an outstanding collection.

BOOKS AND ACCESSORIES

A. THE ART OF THE PAPERWEIGHT: SAINT LOUIS

This magnificently illustrated history of Saint Louis paperweights is the first in a series by Paperweight Press chronicling the outstanding contemporary paperweight manufacturers. The text was prepared by Gerard Ingold, the Commercial Director of Saint Louis, and edited by Lawrence H. Selman and Linda Pope-Selman.

The Saint Louis Archives graciously provided information and illustrations concerning the company's early history and its involvement in paperweight production during the classic period. The book also features information and historical anecdotes about many of the famous collectors who kept the interest in paperweights alive during the years (1865-1952) when manufacturing had ceased. Of special note is the well-illustrated chapter on the processes involved in paperweight production. The book concludes with a catalogue, complete with full-color photographs, of each limited edition from 1970 to 1981.

Superb photography and a definitive text make this book invaluable to every collector of Saint Louis and other fine paperweights. The first edition is limited to 3000 numbered copies. Hardbound, $49.50.

B. SULPHIDES, THE ART OF CAMEO INCRUSTATION

Paperweight scholar and historian Paul Jokelson presents a thorough treatise on the history and art of encasing cameos in crystal, one of the oldest and most fascinating of all paperweight styles. The 159-page book is lavishly illustrated and has its own protective slipcase. Hardbound edition, $9.00.

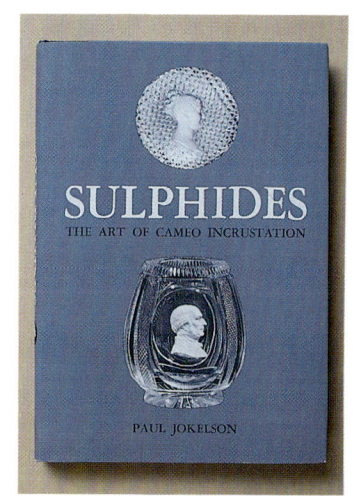

C. FLORA IN GLASS

A 1981 exhibition catalogue of artist Paul Stankard's work over the past ten years. Seventy-one paperweights are illustrated in full color. Hardbound, $32.50.

D. SULFURES ET BOULES PRESSE-PAPIERS

This small, informative guide to paperweights and paperweight-related objects, with French text by Edith Mannoni, is lavishly illustrated in full color. $15.00.

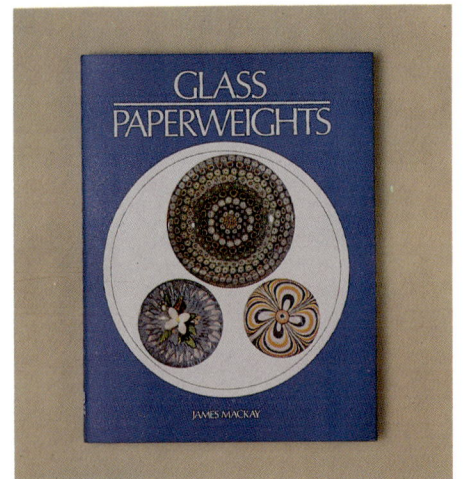

E. GLASS PAPERWEIGHTS

This newly issued edition of James Mackay's well writen manuscript illustrates the origins and history of paperweights. This interesting and informative 110-page book is available in paperback, $8.95, and hardbound, $15.95.

F. CATALOGUING KIT

Excellent for both beginning and experienced collectors, this kit includes printed catalogue cards, self-adhesive labels, an information handbook, and file box. The system is designed to simplify cataloguing and record keeping and provides a complete reference for insurance records and verifications of authenticity. $15.00.

G. LUCITE PAPERWEIGHT STANDS

These lucite stands display large and small paperweights alike, at just the right angle with balanced support. Minimum order of six stands, $15.00; each additional stand, $2.50.

H. CORNING EXHIBITION JIGSAW PUZZLE

The Corning Museum of Glass has authorized their poster design to be used as a jigsaw puzzle of over 600 interlocking pieces. When assembled, this colorful, family fun activity measures 18" x 24". $10.00.

COLLECTORS' PAPERWEIGHTS

I. 1977 PCA BULLETIN

Articles in this edition of the Bulletin include: "Paperweights at Smith College Museum," a piece which highlights rare American and French weights; "Homage to Madame Colette," Gerard Ingold's recollections of this famous French collector; "Robert and Ray Banford," the story behind the artists; and a special on "New Paul Joseph Stankard Orchids." $15.00.

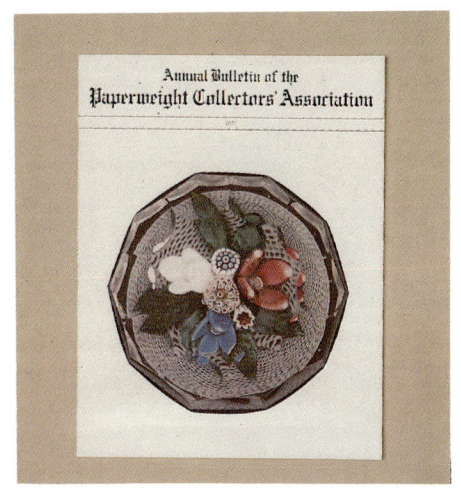

J. 1978 PCA BULLETIN

Featured in this Bulletin are: "Our 25th Anniversary," a note by Paul Jokelson; "The Paperweight Collection of the Hon. A. Houghton," fifteen pages by Dwight Lanmon; "Jewels of Glass from a Captain's Sea Chest," a look at rare weights from a private collection; "Debbie Tarsitano: The Ultimate Challenge," Debbie's start in weight making; "Le Rendezvous à St. Louis," the Selmans' account of their trip to the Saint Louis factory in preparation for the book, The Art of the Paperweight, Saint Louis.

K. 1979 PCA BULLETIN

Among the highlights of this edition are articles such as: "French Millefiori Close-Up," a discussion with photos of typical Baccarat, Clichy, and Saint Louis canes; "The Crystal Garden," paperweights by Delmo and Debbie Tarsitano; an article entitled "Birds . . . and Rick Ayotte;" "Orient and Flume, Iridescence and Beyond;" and a feature on "Paperweight Restoration," by George Kulles. $20.00.

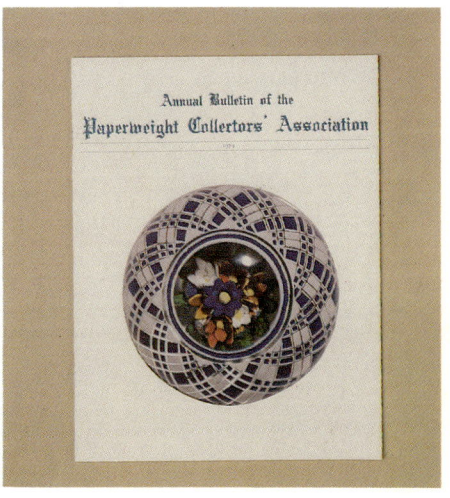

L. 1980 PCA BULLETIN

The following articles are included in this edition: "Glass from the Strauss Collection," by Dwight Lanmon; "Investment Potential of Paperweights," which charts rising prices in paperweights from 1950 to 1980; "The Beauty of Bacchus;" "The Flame Burns Bright," about the Kontes Brothers and their weights; and "Whitefriars Then and Now," the history of Whitefriars. $20.00.

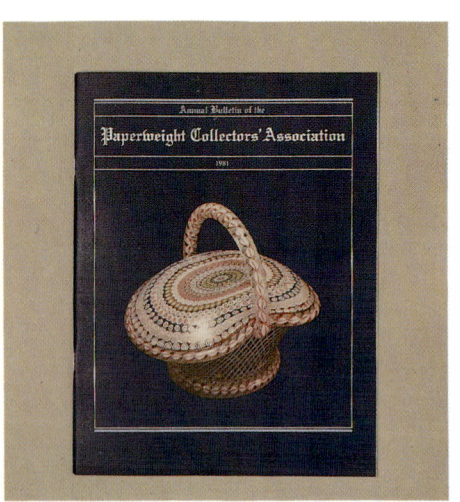

M. 1981 PCA BULLETIN

Featured in this Bulletin are the following articles: "A Pantin Discovery;" "The Paperweight Artistry of Victor Trabucco;" "Paperweights in Needlepoint;" "The Martin Kayser Paperweight;" "Convention 1981;" "The Art of Paperweight: Saint Louis." $20.00.

N. 1982 PCA BULLETIN

The following articles are included in this issue: "Hitherto Unpublished 1982;" "NY/NJ State Chapter PCA visits the Vandermark/Merrit Glass Studio;" "Sulphides—The Art of Cameo Incrustation;" "In Memory of F. Regnault Fairchild and His Paperweight Collection;" "The Collection of Dr. Leon Darnis;" "Ayotte's Glasscapes—Painting With Glass;" "An Unrecorded Sulphide Collection;" "A Collection in Beautiful Balmy Barbados." $20.00.

CONTEMPORARY PAPERWEIGHTS

CONTEMPORARY FACTORIES AND STUDIO ARTISTS

Arranging lampwork petals on a template.

In the 1950s, Paul Jokelson, an importer and avid paperweight enthusiast, approached the glass factories of Baccarat and Saint Louis and urged them to revive the classic art of paperweight production.

Paperweights had not been produced in significant numbers for more than 80 years, and glass artisans at the two factories were faced with the difficult and challenging task of rediscovering the almost lost techniques of paperweight making. Once they succeeded, interest in the contemporary weights led to further production and experimentation.

Since then, a number of glass factories have joined Baccarat and Saint Louis in producing modern paperweights. Cristal D'Albret of France, "J" Glass, Perthshire and Caithness of Scotland, and others utilize traditional techniques and classical motifs while exploring exciting new possibilities in design and technology.

With the renewed interest in paperweights, a number of individual glass workers have also been encouraged to experiment with designs and techniques and produce paperweights on their own.

Arranging millefiori canes on a template.

Many of these artisans gained their skill and expertise in glass by working as scientific and industrial glassblowers, in factories producing decorative glass, or as novelty glassmakers.

The major technical difference between paperweights made by studio artists and those produced in factories is the origin of the glass. Studio artists work with solid glass rods, which they purchase commercially, melt down, and shape over a small gas burner or "torch." The factories create their own glass in large industrial vats. A pontil rod is dipped in to collect the "gather," and the molten glass is formed and shaped.

From a design perspective, most contemporary studio artists are expanding on traditional styles and motifs and creating their own unique designs rather than strictly imitating the traditional French weights of the classic period.

Both the contemporary factories and the studio artists have created the paperweight renaissance of the last 20 years. Their work represents an exciting new generation of paperweights.

RICK AYOTTE

Rick Ayotte is unique among paperweight artists in that he features birds exclusively. A native of Nashua, New Hampshire, Rick's avid interest in ornithology began at an early age. As a boy, he charted migratory bird groups, studied their food and eating habits, and sculpted life-size birds from wood.

After studying at Lowell Technological Institute, Ayotte worked as a scientific glassblower. During that time he also began to create novelty glass items, and in 1970 started Ayotte's Artistry in Glass, a company that specialized in glassware gifts.

In 1976, Ayotte's friend and colleague, paperweight artist Paul Stankard, led him to experiment with paperweight production for the first time. Paperweights offered Ayotte the opportunity to combine his expertise in glass, his design creativity, and his long-time interest in ornithology.

Through extensive research and planning, Ayotte achieves a sense of realism and life in his birds and in his natural environments—qualities which make his paperweights distinctive and of great interest to collectors.

Each paperweight is signed in script with "Ayotte," the number of the weight, and the year. Editions are between 25 and 75 pieces. Color grounds and foliage may vary slightly within a limited edition.

1. RICK AYOTTE

Clusters of grapes and delicate pale green vines surround this stunning yellow-throated vireo. Constructed in two layers, a process which creates a sense of depth and realism, this compound weight is limited to 50 pieces. $400.

2. RICK AYOTTE

Bright orange sumac berries tempt a handsome brown thrasher in this well-crafted lampwork design set on a sky blue ground. This compound weight is part of a limited edition of 50 pieces. $400.

3. RICK AYOTTE

The painted bunting, one of the most brilliantly colored birds in North America, is masterfully captured in this Ayotte weight. Limited to 50 pieces. $350.

4. RICK AYOTTE

This attractive magnolia warbler with its characteristic bright yellow breast is perched amidst lush raspberries. A compound, or two-layer weight set in clear crystal, this work is signed and limited to 50 weights. $400.

5. RICK AYOTTE

Two finely crafted house sparrows, a species familiar to many, are featured against a white ground. The Ayotte signature appears in script and the weight is limited to 50 pieces. $350.

6. RICK AYOTTE

A large snowy owl, perched on a pine branch, is silhouetted against the moonlit sky in this dramatic weight by Rick Ayotte. Signed in script on the side and limited to 75 pieces. $400.

10. BACCARAT

Three richly colored rings of millefiori canes encircle a fresh yellow lampwork flower and bud in this stunning design set on a translucent purple ground. Signed "B1981" in a white cane at the edge of the weight. $495.

11. BACCARAT

Two graceful blue and white flowers with several buds and well-formed leaves rest on a swirling white latticinio ground in this enchanting weight by Baccarat. Limited to 300 pieces, this weight is signed and dated in a cane near the base of the stem. $312.

12. BACCARAT

This charming scattered millefiori weight presents a colorful array of complex canes on a fine lacy ground. Signed and dated in a cane. $310.

13. BACCARAT

Circles of elegant millefiori canes float suspended in this pristine, exceptionally beautiful weight entitled "Couronne." The signature is etched on the base. $145.

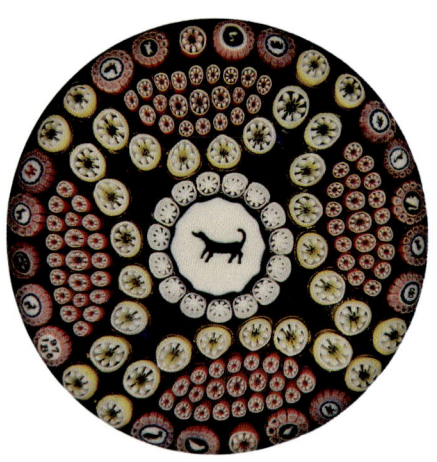

14. BACCARAT

A charming Gridel silhouette cane of a dog is surrounded by patterned millefiori and a number of smaller Gridel animal canes in this enchanting Baccarat weight. Limited to 350 pieces. $275.

15. BACCARAT

Centered on a large deer silhouette cane, this attractive panel weight is divided by graceful silhouette cane spokes featuring all eighteen animals of Baccarat's Gridel series. Signed and dated, this piece is limited to 350. $180.

16. BACCARAT

This finely detailed bust of Thomas Jefferson, the third president of the United States, was sculpted by Gilbert Poillerat for Baccarat. This handsome weight, limited to 594 pieces, is also available with other grounds. $350.

17. BACCARAT

Enhanced by a dramatic red and white overlay, this classic portrait of George Washington was fashioned by Gilbert Poillerat. Limited to an edition of 200. $450. (Regular edition of 1182, $325.)

18. BACCARAT

In this series of sulphide weights, Baccarat commemorates the ancient signs of the zodiac with a series of finely sculpted ceramic cameos set against a deep blue ground and encased in faceted crystal. Grounds may vary. $125.

19. BACCARAT

This distinguished sculpture of Martin Luther was created by Gilbert Poillerat, the artist responsible for reviving the lost art of making sulphides. Grounds may vary in color and cutting. Limited to 607. $325.

20. BACCARAT

This exquisite sulphide illustrates the three-dimensionality Gilbert Poillerat has achieved in his sculpture. Featuring Queen Elizabeth and H.R.H. the Duke of Edinburgh, this weight, which commemorates the coronation, was one of the first modern sulphides produced by Baccarat. Limited to 1492 pieces. $350. (Overlay edition, limited to 195. $450.)

21. BACCARAT

This magnum-size oval weight celebrates the spectacular sixty-foot-high portraits of George Washington, Thomas Jefferson, Abraham Lincoln, and Theodore Roosevelt which are sculpted on the side of Mount Rushmore. Attractively encased in a red and white double overlay and set on a blue ground, this weight is limited to 1000 pieces. $400.

22. BACCARAT

This well-modeled cameo was created in honor of Queen Elizabeth's jubilee anniversary. Sculpted by Gilbert Poillerat, the cameo is set on a regal, amethyst-colored ground and encircled by a ring of millefiori including five Clichy-type roses. Limited to 500 pieces. $500.

23. BACCARAT

First in the series commemorating American presidents, this distinguished portrait of Dwight D. Eisenhower was created by Gilbert Poillerat. The weight is faceted and set on a brilliant clear fan-cut base. Grounds may vary. Limited to 1389 pieces. $400.

24. BACCARAT

This magnificent close pack millefiori weight features a rich assortment of complex canes interspersed with silhouette canes depicting the signs of the zodiac. Signed and dated. $465.

RAY AND BOB BANFORD

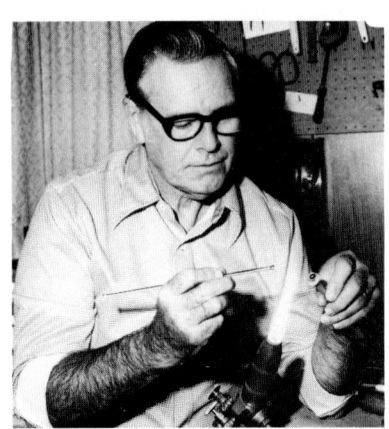

Glass artists Ray and Bob Banford, father and son, have been making French-style paperweights since 1971. The two, who share a workshop behind their home in Hammonton, New Jersey, draw upon each other's expertise but work independently, creating their own designs and functioning as individual craftsmen.

Ray's interest in glass began when he and his wife visited the Corning Museum of Glass and the workshop of an elderly Czechoslovakian glassmaker, Adolph Macho. Ray became fascinated with glass and the glassmaking process, and when Adolph Macho retired, he bought the glassmaker's equipment and began a new career. In addition to paperweights, Ray creates glass buttons and pendants and tends to the business of his and Bob's production.

Bob's glass career began when he received a torch from his parents as a high school graduation gift. With it he began experimenting, first by making ships and carousels of spun glass, then with the challenge of lampwork and paperweight production. Bob's complex lampwork motifs, which include flowers, insects, and reptiles, are realistic and consistently well-designed. His work is displayed at Wheaton Village, the Corning Museum of Glass, and the Smithsonian Institution.

Bob signs his weights with a red, white, and blue "B" initial cane. Ray uses the same initial cane, but in black and white.

25. BOB BANFORD

A brilliant, well-designed lampwork bouquet centers around a traditional purple and yellow pansy in this stunning weight set on a clear waffle cut base. Signed with a "B" cane at the base of the stems. $1440.

26. RAY BANFORD

Two stately iris blooms and a single bud are captured in sparkling clear crystal. Ray Banford's signature cane appears near the base of the stem. $450.

27. RAY BANFORD

This unusual weight features five purple lampwork irises set in clear crystal, which is beautifully overlaid with yellow and white and cut in the shape of a basket. $1200.

28. BOB BANFORD

Two fresh white daisies and finely crafted buds are highlighted by a translucent cobalt blue ground. Signed with an initial cane, the top and sides of this attractive weight are faceted and the bottom is "basket cut." $600.

29. RAY BANFORD

Fresh pink and white morning-glories on deep green leafy tendrils climb on a white lampwork trellis. Set in clear crystal over a strawberry cut base, the weight is signed with a "B" cane. $650.

30. BOB BANFORD

In this well-designed weight, a striking red and white double overlay encases a rich blue lampwork flower with a yellow upright stamen. The bottom edge is basket cut and the piece is signed with a "B" cane. $850.

31. BOB BANFORD

A finely crafted traditional purple and yellow pansy with an upright stamen is set on a clear star cut base. Signed with a red, white, and blue "B" cane. $450.

32. BOB BANFORD

An outstanding cobalt-blue star cut base provides the backdrop for a magnificent magenta-colored flower with heart-shaped petals and two delicate buds. Signed with a red, white, and blue "B" cane. $450.

33. BOB BANFORD

This charming white wheatflower with blue spots and an upright yellow center is surrounded by well-formed leaves. The design is set on a clear star cut base and signed in the usual manner. $500.

34. BOB BANFORD

A basket cut base accents a lovely pink flower and a bumblebee with lacy wings. This attractive faceted weight is set on a clear ground and signed with a "B" cane. $600.

35. RAY BANFORD

Irises, morning-glories, and a rose in full bloom make up this lovely lampwork arrangement set in clear faceted crystal. The weight is signed with a black and white signature cane at the base of the bouquet. $600.

36. BOB BANFORD

A star cut cobalt-blue ground forms a radiant background for this yellow spotted wheatflower. Signed with a red, white, and blue "B" cane at the base of the stem. $500.

D'ALBRET

In 1918, Roger Witkind organized the Cristalleries et Verreries de Viannes in Viannes, France. In 1967, Paul Jokelson, president of the Paperweight Collectors' Association, inspired the factory to inaugurate a series of sulphide paperweights under the name of "Cristalleries d'Albret."

Most of the D'Albret cameos were designed and sculpted by Gilbert Poillerat, one of the most well-known and prolific sulphide artists. Born in 1902, Poillerat studied decorative arts in Paris and worked as a sculptor and a professional medal engraver for the French Mint. Before working with D'Albret, Poillerat did extensive sulphide work with Baccarat.

D'Albret sulphides are produced in both regular and overlay editions. All weights of the same subject are finished with identical faceting and the same color or color combination. The base of each weight is acid-etched with a circle of cursive letters reading "CR. D'ALBRET-FRANCE." In addition, each sulphide is signed on the edge of the bust with the name of the subject, the date the sculpture was made, and the initials of the artist.

37. D'ALBRET

This handsome sulphide with a Star of David cut ground commemorates the first Prime Minister of the State of Israel, David Ben Gurion. The weight is faceted overall and has a rich, translucent blue ground. Limited to 750 pieces. $200. (Blue and white double overlay with Star of David cutting in a clear base, limited to 150 pieces, also available. $275.)

38. D'ALBRET

The signing of the 1978 Peace Treaty between Israel and the United Arab Republic is commemorated in this historically significant sulphide depicting Prime Minister Menachem Begin and President Anwar el Sadat. Faceted and set on a translucent amethyst ground, this weight is limited to 600 pieces. $125. (Lavender-and-white overlay edition set on a clear ground and limited to 120 pieces also available. $275.)

39. D'ALBRET

Dr. Albert Schweitzer, the renowned philosopher, missionary doctor, and winner of the Nobel Peace Prize in 1952, is handsomely portrayed in this Cristalleries d'Albret sulphide. Highlighted by fancy cutting and a blue flash overlay, this weight is limited to 200 pieces. $185. (Regular edition limited to 1000. $70.)

40. D'ALBRET

An amber-and-white double overlay enhances Gilbert Poillerat's expressive portrait of Golda Meir, the strong and influential woman who served as Israel's Prime Minister from 1969-1974. This piece is set on a clear ground with Star of David cutting on the base. Limited to 150 pieces. $225. (Regular edition also available, $125. Limited to 850.)

41. D'ALBRET

One of Israel's most noted soldiers and statesmen, Moshe Dayan, is honored in this handsome sulphide by artist Gilbert Poillerat. Dramatically highlighted by a blue-and-white overlay, this well-modeled cameo is featured on a clear ground with Star of David cutting on the base. Limited to 120 pieces. $225. (Regular edition weight, limited to 600 pieces, also available. $125.)

42. D'ALBRET

The French-born American naturalist and painter, James Audubon, is set against a rich translucent blue ground in this finely detailed sulphide by Gilbert Poillerat. Limited to 1000 pieces. $75. (Double overlay edition of 225 is also available. $170.)

43. D'ALBRET

From a sculpture by artist Leo Holmgren, this cameo portrait of H.M. Gustaf VI is issued in a limited edition of 1000. $70.

44. D'ALBRET

In this well-designed sulphide, sculptor Gilbert Poillerat features the Scales of Justice, symbol of balance and fairness in our judicial system. An excellent gift for a friend or a colleague in the legal profession, this sulphide is set on a deep blue ground and faceted overall. Limited to 1000 pieces. $180.

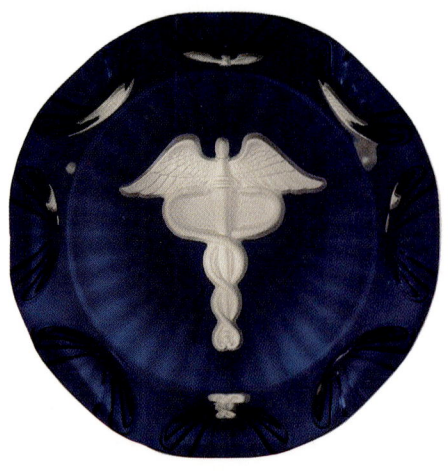

45. D'ALBRET

An ancient symbol of healing, the Caduceus is featured in this finely sculpted sulphide by Gilbert Poillerat. Set on a brilliant cobalt-blue, star cut ground, this elegant weight is the perfect gift for someone in the medical profession. Limited to 1000. $180.

"J" GLASS

"J" Glass, a Scottish factory in Crieff, Perthshire, was founded in 1979 by John Deacons, an experienced and skilled designer who was trained at Edinburgh College of Art and later employed by Perthshire Paperweights. The "J" Glass Company derived its name from an enigmatic "J" signature cane found in certain nineteenth-century Bohemian paperweights.

"J" Glass paperweights are produced in classic millefiori motifs using authentic nineteenth-century colors. The weights also feature floral designs in lampwork and millefiori techniques.

Each edition produced by "J" Glass contains not more than 101 pieces. John Deacons retains one piece from every edition. A blue "J" encircled by the year of manufacture in red, green, and blue is the official signature/date cane of the company. A numbered certificate, which describes the weight and is signed by John Deacons, accompanies each paperweight.

46. "J" GLASS

Inspired by an antique Saint Louis weight, this upright bouquet of lampwork and millefiori flowers is encased in a double rose-and-white overlay. The base is star cut. $350.

47. "J" GLASS

This large, yellow, old-fashioned rose with green leaves is set on a bright cobalt-blue ground. Limited to 101 for 1983. $250.

48. "J" GLASS

This stunning pink and white dahlia fills a three-inch clear weight. The flower is convex and is edged with six variegated green leaves. Limited edition of 101 for 1983. $300.

49. "J" GLASS

A brilliant yellow buttercup floats in clear glass, surrounded by a ring of alternating blue and white millefiori. The stamen is made up of a tiny stardust cane. Limited to 101 for 1983. $250.

50. "J" GLASS

A lampwork bouquet is set into a rose-colored ground. Each of the flower centers is a millefiori cane. Signed with a "J" cane at the base of the stems, this weight is a limited edition of 101. $250.

51. "J" GLASS

Encased in a double yellow over white overlay, this pansy bouquet floats over an unusual cut base. Limited to 101. $325.

52. "J" GLASS

This Christmas weight is a tree with millefiori ornaments set on an upset muslin ground. It is encased in a ruby flash overlay. $285.

53. "J" GLASS

Fragile wild cherry blossoms and buds cling to leafy branches in this stunning clear faceted weight. Limited to 101 pieces. $290.

54. "J" GLASS

A blue and white millefiori garland surrounds a millefiori butterfly. The ground is purple and the weight has one top facet and ten side "finger" facets. Limited to 101. $325.

55. "J" GLASS

An old-fashioned rose and bud are set in clear crystal and surrounded by a single ring of millefiori. The weight is faceted so that there appears to be a second ring around the rose. Limited to 101. $260.

56. "J" GLASS

A single yellow "Bloom in May" is set on a translucent blue ground in this miniature weight. Signed in a cane at the base of the stem and limited to 101. $150.

57. "J" GLASS

Similar to antique primroses, this modern "J" weight is set in clear crystal. The center is a tiny cluster of white stardust canes. $165.

58. "J" GLASS

This miniature weight features a single pink dahlia set on a blue translucent ground. $150.

59. "J" GLASS

A lampwork and latticinio winged dragonfly hovers over a delicate bouquet, set over a clear ground. The weight is faceted and limited to 101 pieces. $325.

60. "J" GLASS

Radiating latticinio spokes are the background for this wild rose and leaves. The signature cane is on the bottom of this weight. $185.

CHARLES KAZIUN

Charles Kaziun's interest in glass began at a very early age when he first saw a family of glass blowers demonstrating their craft at the County Fair in Brockton, Massachusetts. He spent the next six days at the Fair, from 9 o'clock in the morning until 10 o'clock at night, transfixed in front of the glass blowing exhibit, and soon began experimenting at home with a makeshift glass blowing set-up.

Throughout his career, Kaziun has worked as a scientific glassblower as well as experimenting with his own glass designs and techniques. He has innovated a one-man method of millefiori cane production and is an expert at making muslin and swirling latticinio. Besides millefiori paperweights, Kaziun produces a variety of floral motifs such as the pansy, lily, dogwood and morning-glory. He has also created a number of exquisite gold foil inclusions. Perfume bottles, footed miniature weights, and paperweight buttons are also part of his work.

Kaziun weights are signed with a 14-karat-gold "K" and/or a millefiori "K" signature cane integrated into the design.

61. CHARLES KAZIUN

Set on a lovely lace-over-translucent-turquoise ground, this miniature patterned millefiori weight is centered on a colorful millefiori cane which features a silhouette of a tiny red heart. This charming weight is signed with a "K" millefiori cane and a gold foil "K" on the reverse side. $1200.

62. CHARLES KAZIUN

A handsome yellow and black striped snake is featured on a white lace-over-deep-amethyst ground. This intricately designed weight is faceted and signed "K" in a millefiori cane on the underside. $2275.

63. CHARLES KAZIUN

This exquisite patterned millefiori design is set on a deep cobalt-blue ground and handsomely faceted. Signed "K" in the central millefiori cane. $1500.

64. CHARLES KAZIUN

This unusual miniature treasure features a gold foil silhouette of a woman surrounded by five stunning millefiori canes. Set on a rich amethyst ground, this weight is faceted and signed with a gold "K" on the reverse. $1200.

65. CHARLES KAZIUN

An elegant morning-glory on a trellis and a jewel-like gold foil bee are set against a bright turquoise ground in this inventive weight by Charles Kaziun. $1500.

66. CHARLES KAZIUN

An upright spider lily on a lovely opaque-colored ground rests delicately on a clear glass pedestal. This miniature, two-and-one-half-inch high piedouche weight is signed with a gold "K" on the base. Colors may vary. $395.

LUNDBERG STUDIOS

In 1967, James Lundberg, founder of Lundberg Studios, attended one of the first college classes in glassblowing ever offered on the West Coast. Classically trained in ceramics, Lundberg found glass an exciting medium more suited to his temperament and artistic vision. After graduating with a degree in art and studying glass techniques throughout Europe, Lundberg joined together with a handful of artisans and created a small backyard glass studio in San Jose, California.

In 1972, Lundberg Studios began to produce paperweights for L.H. Selman Ltd., and moved their operation to Davenport, California, a small town south of San Francisco. Located in a refurbished bakery, their studio includes four melting furnaces, five glory holes, and two torch working areas for paperweights, as well as a complete grinding machine and lamp shop. The studio is staffed by several artists operating in the Renaissance tradition, each contributing his or her special skills to the glass process.

Lundberg Studios is well known for its exquisite Tiffany-style paperweights, vases, jewelry, lamps, and tiles. They also produce very fine clear weights featuring motifs such as birds, butterflies, flowers, seascapes, and astronomical designs.

Each Lundberg piece is signed with the studio name, artist's name, date, and number. As of July, 1980, all Lundberg glass items are accompanied by a certificate of authenticity.

67. LUNDBERG STUDIOS

A long-time symbol of peace and tranquility, this majestic white crane is set in full flight against a midnight blue ground. Signed and dated. $145.

68. LUNDBERG STUDIOS

Delicately fluted pink petal and spring green leaves surround an upright millefiori stamen in this ruffle-edged camellia designed by Lundberg Studios. Signed by the artist and studio on the base and limited to 250 pieces. $145.

69. LUNDBERG STUDIOS

Set against a dramatic cobalt-blue ground, a pale yellow lampwork butterfly hovers near graceful shoots of fresh bamboo. Dated and signed by Lundberg Studios and the artist. $145.

70. LUNDBERG STUDIOS

A deep, mysterious, iridescent ground sets off an undersea world of jellyfish, pale green strands of seaweed, and a delicate tropical fish, by Lundberg Studios. $135.

71. LUNDBERG STUDIOS

Pink dogwood blossoms are set in clear crystal over an encased iridescent ground. $110.

72. LUNDBERG STUDIOS

A pink and deep burgundy fuchsia flower and bud fall from a graceful leafy vine in this exquisite lampwork design featured on a cobalt-blue ground and encased in clear crystal. Signed by the studio and artist on the base, and limited to 250 pieces. $135.

ORIENT & FLUME

In 1972, Orient & Flume started out as a two-person operation in Chico, California. Since then, the staff has grown to twenty persons, including artists, clerical, managerial, and shipping personnel.

Deriving its name from bordering cross streets, Orient & Flume operates as a cooperative studio. Designs are developed by members of the staff, who pool their ideas and incorporate them into the final product. Through this designing technique, Orient & Flume has developed a unique style and a reputation for consistently fine quality work.

Orient & Flume's early weights are characterized by art nouveau motifs, iridescence, and surface decoration. Currently, they have combined art nouveau design elements with graceful traditional paperweight techniques to create a distinctive modern style. Their work includes millefiori cane flowers, classic florals, butterflies, and dragonflies. They have also expanded their designs to jewelry, lampshades, and stained glass.

Each Orient & Flume paperweight is signed, dated, and numbered on the base and is issued with a certificate of authenticity.

73. ORIENT & FLUME

A colorful spring bouquet decorates the surface of this stunning iridescent blue weight. Colors and flowers may vary slightly in each weight. $125.

74. ORIENT & FLUME

A large three-color marbrie weight is topped off by a silhouette cane. The new issues will be a kangaroo silhouette or complex millefiori. Colors may vary. $150.

75. ORIENT & FLUME

Elegant dogwood blossoms grace the surface of this iridescent gold weight by Orient & Flume. Signed, numbered, and dated on the base. $90.

PERTHSHIRE PAPERWEIGHTS

Perthshire Paperweights of Crieff, Scotland, which grew out of Vasart Glass and its predecessor Strathearn Glass, was formed in 1969 by Stuart Drysdale, a country lawyer and businessman. Perthshire's first factory was located in an old schoolhouse. Within two years, the tremendous success of their business in the field of limited edition collectors' paperweights enabled them to open a new factory in Crieff. At that time, Perthshire was the only factory in the world devoted entirely to the production of millefiori paperweights and related objects.

Perthshire's "metal" (glass) is produced in a one-ton tank on the weekends for work during the following week. Almost all of the raw materials used in its manufacture are from local sources.

Millefiori designs are created by the glassworkers themselves, who are encouraged to experiment with colors and motifs.

The factory issues three series of paperweights: special limited editions, which are produced only once, regular limited editions, which are repeated each year in small numbers, and unlimited editions.

All Perthshire weights are signed with one of three styles of signature/date canes. The yearly limited editions since 1969 contain an alphabet cane beginning with "A" for that year to "O" in 1983, embedded in the top design of the paperweight. Other weights carry a "P" cane, with the year of manufacture either in the motif or on the bottom of the weight. Others are identified by a single "P" cane within the design.

76. PERTHSHIRE

A brilliant pink pompon with green leaves surrounded by a ruby flash overlay and ground form a stunning color arrangement in this well-designed weight. Signed and limited to 300 pieces. $495.

77. PERTHSHIRE

A "P" signature cane makes up the center of a graceful blossom set on a clear strawberry grid cut base. This faceted miniature weight is part of a limited edition of 600. Flowers may vary in color. $200.

78. PERTHSHIRE

Pressed into delicate flutes, the outer glass of this sparkling miniature weight sets off concentric millefiori canes centered around a "P" signature cane. Colors may vary. $50.

79. PERTHSHIRE

Patterned millefiori divided by latticinio spokes make up this handsome two-and-one-half-inch weight. The design, which centers on a "P" signature cane, is set on a translucent ground. Colors and design may vary. $50.

80. PERTHSHIRE

A garland of millefiori circlets surrounds a superb white lampwork flower set on a translucent garnet-colored base. Signed by the factory, this piece is part of a limited edition of 250. $240.

81. PERTHSHIRE

This pristine miniature weight features tiny finely crafted millefiori canes in a star pattern, which is reflected through intricate side faceting. Set on a clear ground, color combinations may vary in this lovely weight, limited to 300 pieces. $250.

PERTHSHIRE PAPERWEIGHTS

82. PERTHSHIRE

This multifaceted weight offers a unique underwater view of aquarium life. Two colorful tropical fish, a seahorse, graceful pink seaweed, a crab, and small shell are featured in this fascinating weight by Perthshire. Limited to 350 pieces. $400.

83. PERTHSHIRE

Panels of millefiori canes separated by latticinio twists radiate from a concentric center. Signed and dated in a cane and set on a translucent ground, this appealing weight is part of a yearly limited edition of 300. Colors may vary. $150.

84. PERTHSHIRE

Unusual side faceting enhances a well-formed lampwork arrangement of acorns and oak leaves set on a delicate cushion of latticinio. This piece is part of a limited edition of 300. $440.

85. PERTHSHIRE

A spray of pale pink flowers with millefiori cane centers is shown on a delicate blue ground. The design is set off by three rows of side facets. Limited to 250. $440.

86. PERTHSHIRE

A graceful flamingo feeds in a cool blue lily pond attractively displayed through a single top facet. Limited to 300 pieces. $190.

87. PERTHSHIRE

A variety of millefiori and colored silhouette canes are scattered on a cushion of finely spun latticinio threads. A cane bearing the factory signature is included in the center. $135. (Miniature available. $95.)

88. PERTHSHIRE

An outstanding assortment of close packed millefiori canes is magnificently displayed through a rich amber-over-white double overlay. Limited to 250 pieces. $440.

89. PERTHSHIRE

Five colored silhouette canes depicting nursery rhyme and cartoon characters playfully encircle a close packed millefiori center. This very special Perthshire weight is edged with a ring of millefiori canes and set on a cobalt-blue ground. Limited to an edition of 300. $315.

90. PERTHSHIRE

This jewel-like bouquet, with a blue-and-white double overlay and fancy cut sides, is set on a star cut base. Part of a limited edition of 300. $495.

91. PERTHSHIRE

This charming two-and-one-half-inch patterned millefiori weight features a selection of finely crafted millefiori divided by colorful twisted latticinio canes. Signed in the center with a "P" cane, no two weights are exactly alike in color. $40. (Larger version with slightly different arrangement of canes. $57.50.)

92. PERTHSHIRE

In this unique and fascinating weight, three lampwork bumblebees appear as a swarm through clear crystal which has been faceted overall. Set on a strawberry grid cut base, this magnum weight is limited to 200 pieces. $540.

93. PERTHSHIRE

A gentian blue flower on horizontal latticinio is distinctively framed by a border of blue and white millefiori canes. This signed weight is limited to 400 pieces. $265.

SAINT LOUIS

Cristalleries de Saint Louis, one of the three great French factories during the classical era of paperweights (1840-1860), resumed paperweight production in 1953 after a lapse of nearly 100 years. Located in the Alsace-Lorraine region of France, Saint Louis is considered one of the foremost glass factories in the world today.

Saint Louis produces millefiori, lampwork, and sulphide paperweights, many patterned after its superb nineteenth-century designs. In the classical tradition, Saint Louis creates mushroom overlay, pinwheel, and piedouche weights. In addition, the factory has added distinctive modern techniques such as gold inclusions and magnum-encased double overlays. Saint Louis is also well known for distinctive paperweight-related objects such as candlesticks, newel posts, shot glasses and handcoolers.

Modern Saint Louis weights are signed with the initials "SL" and the date within a cane, and each weight is accompanied by a certificate of authenticity.

94. SAINT LOUIS

These lilies of the valley on a ruby ground are part of a limited edition of 200. This weight is modeled after an antique Clichy that sold for a large sum at auction recently. $380.

95. SAINT LOUIS

"Basket of Flowers" inspired by the famous antique Clichy weight. Fine millefiori canes represent tiny flowers, latticinio and spiral twists form the basket. Limited to 250, a few green pieces are also available. $840.

96. SAINT LOUIS

An upright fountain bouquet of three-dimensional lampwork blooms is seen through a complementary rose-pink and white double overlay. This piece, which will be issued during 1983, is part of a limited edition of 200. $770.

97. SAINT LOUIS

This stunning blue and white four-flower bouquet set in clear faceted crystal is reminiscent of the highly regarded Baccarat four-flower bouquet. This piece, which will be issued in 1983, is part of a limited edition of 200. $460.

98. SAINT LOUIS

In this classically lovely weight entitled "Amour," a delicate Cupid sulphide is encircled by a garland of blue forget-me-nots with millefiori centers. This piece is especially interesting in that it combines a sulphide with millefiori canes and lampwork, on an encased colored ground. Limited to 400. $385.

99. SAINT LOUIS

White stardust canes make up this carpet ground with scattered millefiori in many colors. This weight is limited to 200 for 1982, and signed in a pink cane "SL1982." $400.

100. SAINT LOUIS

A single blue and white flower rests on top of a latticinio bubble, bringing the flower almost to the surface of the weight. It is signed and dated in the center of the flower in a cane. $430.

101. SAINT LOUIS

Luscious ripe strawberries are set on a bed of white latticinio in this limited edition of 200 for 1982. This weight is faceted with one top window and five side facets. $430.

102. SAINT LOUIS

A carpet ground of blue millefiori with dainty red and white floral centers makes up this edition of 200. $400.

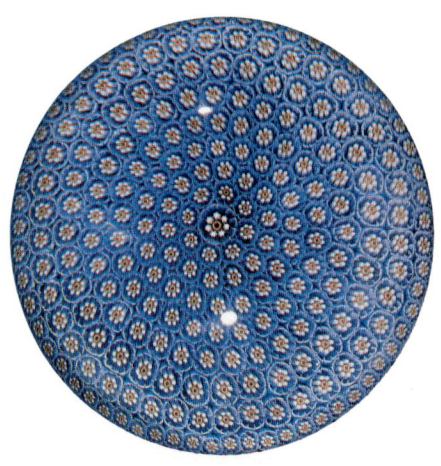

103. SAINT LOUIS

A lively bouquet of colorful lampwork blooms is set in sparkling clear crystal. Signed "SL1981" in the center of the open white flower, this piece is limited to 250. $560.

104. SAINT LOUIS

A "Valentine Bouquet" made up of delicate lampwork flowers and a millefiori heart is set on a romantic mauve pink ground. This very special weight will be issued in 1983 as a limited edition of 200. $440.

105. SAINT LOUIS

A splendid yellow lampwork rose and bud with emerald green stems and leaves is set against a cobalt-blue ground. This weight will be issued during 1983 as a limited edition of 200. $390.

106. SAINT LOUIS

A delightful upright bouquet is enhanced by a technically difficult encased triple overlay. This extraordinary magnum-sized weight will be issued by Saint Louis in 1983. Limited to 50. $2600.

107. SAINT LOUIS

Reminiscent of a rare antique Clichy weight which sold at auction for $50,000, this lovely red-edged convolvulus by Saint Louis is set on a white latticinio bed and encased in faceted crystal. Part of a 1983 limited edition of 200. $440.

108. SAINT LOUIS

This finely detailed lampwork camomile and bud are featured on a dramatic swirling pink latticinio bed. This extraordinary weight will be issued in 1983 as part of a limited edition of 200. $430.

PAUL STANKARD

Paul Stankard started working as a scientific glass technologist almost twenty years ago. It was through this work that he developed many of the highly sophisticated skills and techniques which he has used in creating his floral paperweights. His proficiency and understanding of the material have allowed him to experiment and extend the limits of glass as an artistic medium.

Stankard's weights are meticulously crafted and feature botanically accurate and naturalistically colored floral subjects. Tiny blossoms with delicate stamens, veined leaves, and variegated root systems are presented in exceptionally fine detail.

As much a botanist as an artist, Stankard sketches directly from nature and even keeps specimens of wildflowers in cubes of ice to examine when fresh flowers are not available.

Experimentation is an integral part of Stankard's work. He produces many one-of-a-kind or "experimental" weights in search of the best design, color, and composition. His methods of portraying the three-dimensionality and complexities of a subject are unique and have placed him at the forefront of contemporary glass designers.

His early weights bear either an etched signature on the base or side, or an "S" or "PS" signature cane. His recent work is identified by an "S" signature cane placed at the base of a color ground or on the side of a clear ground.

109. PAUL STANKARD - RICK AYOTTE

Paul Stankard's fresh meadow flower with its cross section of a seed pod and slender stem and leaves, provides the perfect resting place for a colorful rose-breasted grosbeak crafted by Rick Ayotte. Set on a clear ground, this combination weight is signed in script on the side with "Ayotte" and "Stankard," and also contains an "S" cane. $900.

110. PAUL STANKARD

A cobalt blue translucent ground forms the dramatic backdrop for this exquisitely crafted lady's-slipper orchid. $850.

111. PAUL STANKARD

A magnificent "Rose Bouquet" made up of stunning three-dimensional blooms reveals the exceptional artistry and innovation in Paul Stankard's work. $1200.

112. PAUL STANKARD

In this pastel "Spring Bouquet," Paul Stankard features some of his finest lampwork blooms, including purple chive blossoms, yellow bellwort, lily of the valley, and meadowreath. Signed with an "S" cane on the side, this piece is limited to 50 pieces. $900.

113. PAUL STANKARD

In this experimental weight by Paul Stankard, a pair of fresh white daisies with yellow stamens and slender leaves and stems are set in clear crystal. $600.

114. PAUL STANKARD

Shaded pale pink blooms with delicately crafted yellow-and-orange stamens make up this superb weight entitled "Tea Rose," created exclusively for L.H. Selman Ltd. in a limited edition of 50. Signed with an "S" cane on the side, each weight features a slightly different arrangement of flowers and leaves. $850.

115. PAUL STANKARD

In this exquisite brilliant red rose, each stamen is individually constructed and the petals and leaves are carefully enameled to achieve naturalistic coloration. This experimental weight is set in clear crystal and signed by the artist. $600.

116. PAUL STANKARD

In this botanically accurate lampwork design, Paul Stankard reveals the bulb and root system of an exotic blooming arethusa orchid. Featured on a translucent blue ground, this weight is limited to 100 pieces. $750.

117. PAUL STANKARD

An exceptionally beautiful braided bouquet with an array of fresh spring flowers and buds is set on a crystal clear ground. Signed with an "S" cane, the arrangement varies slightly with each weight. $1000.

"Working in the studio creating paperweights over the last thirteen years has been very challenging and a fulfilling experience. I've always wished I could have invented the paperweight art form. In 1980, I started experimenting with the hope of developing a new effect; by re-arranging the glass flower making techniques, I discovered new results which I titled 'glass botanicals.' The glass botanicals, which I feel very strongly towards, are a new way of looking at the glass flowers encased in crystal. I would like to think that the glass botanical sculpture could become second generation paperweights in the French floral tradition."

Paul Stankard

118. PAUL STANKARD
THE BOTANICAL PAPERWEIGHT

A new and innovative work, the rose botanical breaks through the size and shape constraints of the traditional paperweight. This elegant glass sculpture reveals the magnificence of the flowering bush as well as the hidden beauties of the root structure below the ground. The rose botanical will be produced in an edition of not more than 30. Each piece is signed, dated and numbered. Due to the complexity of the design, the botanicals are individually priced from $3,000 to $4,000.

Detail of a rose

DELMO AND DEBBIE TARSITANO

Delmo and Debbie Tarsitano, father and daughter, have been creating outstanding lampwork paperweights since 1976. Working in their studio on Long Island, surrounded by Debbie's rose garden and Del's vegetable garden, each of them originates their own designs and set-ups and assists one another in the final stages of the encasement process.

The combination of Debbie's formal training in art at Hofstra University and Del's technical expertise and interest in nature, has contributed greatly to the Tarsitanos' success in creating realistic and dimensional paperweights. Del features colorful fruits, vegetables, and reptiles in his weights, while Debbie produces well-balanced, finely-designed floral compositions.

Their paperweights have been shown at the Corning Museum of Glass, the Metropolitan Museum of Art, the Bergstrom Art Center, and the Art Institute of Chicago.

Tarsitano weights are produced in a very limited number and are neither dated nor numbered. Before 1980, their weights were signed with an initial "T" cane. Their weights are now identified by a "DT" cane placed at the edge of the motif, or under a leaf.

119. DELMO TARSITANO

A finely sculpted, bright green salamander with yellow shaded sides is featured on a naturalistic sandy ground. Signed with a "DT" cane by the tail. $500. (A pale green, mottled salamander is also available. $535.)

120. DEBBIE TARSITANO

Three bumblebees with lacy wings surround a large sunny zinnia in this cheerful design set on a clear grid cut base. Signed "DT" in a cane. $600.

121. DELMO TARSITANO

Reminiscent of the classic French reptile weights, an unusual brilliant red snake with lighter shaded spots is set on a rich sandy ground. The "DT" signature cane appears near the tail of the snake. $600. (Green snake also available.)

122. DEBBIE TARSITANO

Blooming on a leaf covered branch, four pink striped blossoms with delicate yellow stamens are set on a clear star cut base. Signed with a "DT" signature cane. $525.

123. DEBBIE TARSITANO

Three blue gentians and a bud are set over a strawberry cut clear ground. This weight is inspired by the antique Baccarat gentian weights. $750.

124. DEBBIE TARSITANO

A mix of fanciful flowers set in clear crystal makes up this attractive floral bouquet miniature by Debbie Tarsitano. Each weight may feature slightly different blooms. $330.

125. DEBBIE TARSITANO

This miniature red and white primrose is set on a star cut clear crystal base, which is elegantly reflected in the side faceting. $330.

126. DEBBIE TARSITANO

This breathtaking magnum-size weight presents a carpet of colorful blooms finely crafted by Debbie Tarsitano. The design, which includes a variety of flowers such as pansies, a primrose, and a wheatflower, is signed "DT" in a cane near the side of the weight. $2400.

127. DELMO TARSITANO

A superbly designed cluster of ripe red strawberries and delicate white blossoms is effectively set in clear crystal. $600.

128. DELMO TARSITANO

This miniature "honeycomb" faceted weight features three lampwork cherries on stems with green leaves set on a sparkling, star cut base. Signed with the initials "DT" in a cane under one of the leaves. $450.

129. DEBBIE TARSITANO

A charming blue basket with a twisted cane handle displays an arrangement of bright pansies with delicate sprigs of lily of the valley. Set over a clear ground and signed by the artist. $525.

130. DEBBIE TARSITANO - PAUL YSART

Complex millefiori canes created by master paperweight artist Paul Ysart encircle an exquisite spotted wheatflower by Debbie Tarsitano. This charming combination weight, set in clear crystal, is signed with both a "PY" cane and a "DT" cane. $800.

131. DELMO TARSITANO

A sparkling, star cut clear base and three rows of side faceting highlight this well-formed, ripe, fuzzy peach by Delmo Tarsitano. $650.

132. DEBBIE TARSITANO

Two bold "tropical sunflowers" with large full stamens create a distinctive composition set in clear crystal. A "DT" signature cane appears under one of the green leaves. $525.

133. DELMO TARSITANO

A richly colored strawberry and two snow-white blossoms are surrounded by well-formed leaves in this miniature weight set on a crystal clear ground. $300.

VICTOR TRABUCCO

Victor Trabucco became interested in glass in 1974, when he first saw a lampworker spinning ships and animals from heated glass. He began to ask questions, and although the glassblower was secretive about his work, Trabucco decided to pursue the interest on his own.

A steelworker by trade, with no formal training in art or scientific glassblowing, Trabucco began to study and experiment with glass. Working in a basement studio in his home near Buffalo, New York, he began producing novelty pieces for shops in his area. Over the years he has created a number of award-winning glass sculptures, many of which have been commissioned by large corporations.

In 1977, after examining several antique French paperweights, Trabucco began to experiment with paperweight making. He became fascinated with melding delicate lampwork arrangements with solid crystal, and after a year of trial and error he successfully mastered the technique. His sculptural expertise and attention to color, design, and glass quality, have made him an important contributor to the paperweight renaissance.

Trabucco produces approximately 100-150 clear crystal-enclosed weights per year. Each edition consists of 25-75 pieces. His weights are signed with a "T" cane; his signature and the date are also etched on the side of each weight.

134. VICTOR TRABUCCO

Bright red blooms are arranged with a pale pink flower and bud in this aesthetically pleasing bouquet encased in clear crystal. Signed and numbered on the side, this weight is limited to 50 pieces. $350.

135. VICTOR TRABUCCO

African black-eyed Susans with delicate upright stamens are surrounded by leafy green tendrils in this bright and sunny weight. Signed "VT" in a white cane on the underside of a leaf, and limited to 50 pieces. $325.

136. VICTOR TRABUCCO

Entitled "Nature in Ice," this fresh and elegant composition features a lush ripe strawberry on a blossoming vine. Set in sparkling crystal, this sculpture stands upright on a flat base. Signed, numbered, and limited to 50 pieces. $450.

137. VICTOR TRABUCCO

Two pale pink camellias and a delicate hanging bud are featured in this exquisite design set on a clear ground. Limited to 50 pieces, the number is etched on the side of each weight. $375.

138. VICTOR TRABUCCO

In this delightful weight, a lavender and blue "forget-me-not bouquet" sparkles in clear crystal. Signed by the artist. $300.

139. VICTOR TRABUCCO

A spray of exotic pale pink dendrobium orchids bloom on a flowing green stem encased in clear crystal. Signed and numbered, this weight is part of a limited edition of 50. $350.

FRANCIS WHITTEMORE

As a child, Francis Whittemore began experimenting with a Bunsen burner and glass rods after seeing the famous Blaschka glass flower collection at Harvard University. By the time he was in high school, Whittemore had become so proficient that he was supplying goblets, decanters, and small animal figurines to local gift shops.

After high school, Whittemore studied at Harvard University before entering the military. After his discharge in 1946, he worked as a technical glassblower for sixteen years and then became a teacher at the Salem County Vocational Technical Institute in New Jersey. There, in 1962, a student's question about paperweight manufacturing techniques led Whittemore to look into the subject.

In his early weights, Whittemore concentrated on replicating the deceptively simple-looking Millville rose. He then began working in the classic French paperweight style. He also incorporated his designs into perfume bottles, glasses, and other paperweight-related objects.

Whittemore, who has worked as a consultant for Baccarat, started his own business in 1968. He specializes in single flower motifs and periodically creates unusual botanical designs.

All Francis Whittemore weights are signed with a "W" signature cane.

140. FRANCIS WHITTEMORE

A classic red rose, symbol of beauty and perfection, is encased in clear crystal in this miniature weight by Francis Whittemore. Signed with a "W" cane at the base of the stem. $320.

141. FRANCIS WHITTEMORE

A fragile pink wild rose with an upright yellow stamen and a graceful, partially opened blossom are encased in clear crystal. This lovely miniature weight is signed "W" at the base of the stem. $350.

142. FRANCIS WHITTEMORE

This precious miniature weight features delicate violets on graceful green stems set in clear crystal. Signed with a "W" cane. $320.

PAUL YSART

 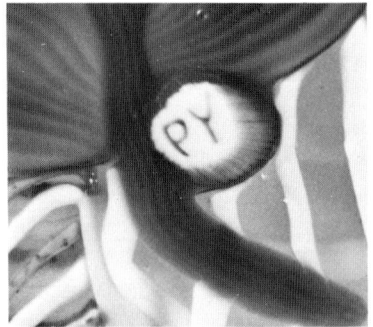

Master glass artist Paul Ysart was born in Barcelona, Spain, in 1904. Both his father and grandfather were glassblowers, and early on, Paul and his three brothers were introduced to the glass profession. The Ysart family migrated to Scotland, and in 1922 the four brothers joined the Moncrieff Limited Glassworks in Perth, Scotland. It was during his years at Perth that Paul became interested in paperweight making.

As early as 1938, Paul was creating quality weights. Although his brothers branched off and created their own firm, Paul remained with Moncrieff and during his years there produced some of the finest paperweights made since the nineteenth century.

In 1963, Ysart went to work at Caithness Glass in Wick, Scotland. Although his position was personnel officer, he continued to create paperweights on his own time. Between 1963 and 1970, he produced over twenty different types of weights.

In 1971, Ysart started the Paul Ysart Glass Company in Wick, Scotland. He produced only paperweights and other glass objects in very limited editions until he retired in 1979.

Ysart's millefiori weights range from random to patterned schemes set on clear, colored, or lace grounds. His flowers are generally of the clematis type with leaves and stems but usually no buds, and are featured on jasper, colored, latticinio, or pulled cane grounds. Other weights feature butterflies, lacy or decorated snakes, dragonflies, and swimming fish.

Most Ysart weights are signed with a small "PY" cane either in the design or on the base.

143. PAUL YSART

A well-designed rose and bud with emerald green leaves and stems is set on a dark opaque ground. Signed with a "PY" cane at the base of the stem. $600.

144. PAUL YSART

A bright blue and white blossom with a stunning orange and yellow millefiori stamen is surrounded by a ring of jewel-like millefiori canes in this beautiful weight created by master glass artist Paul Ysart. Set on a translucent blue ground, this weight is unsigned. $375.

145. PAUL YSART

A popular motif in antique paperweights, this handsome spotted snake coiled on an opaque red ground was fashioned by Paul Ysart. Signed with a "PY" cane at the end of the tail. $550.

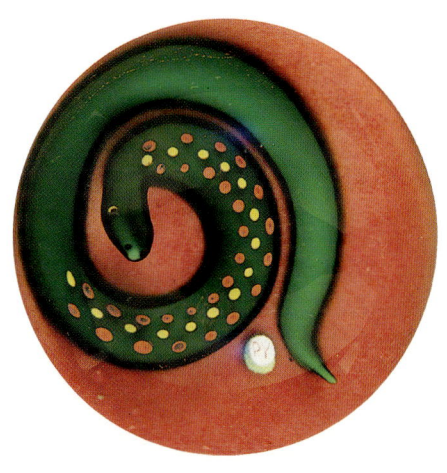

MISCELLANEOUS

146. DAVID LOTTON

Pink flowers and vines are on the surface of this iridescent weight. Signed with signature and year in script on the base. $100.

147. WHITEFRIARS

Featured amidst lavish concentric circles of millefiori is a lovely Star of David made up of tiny, fine, blue and white millefiori canes. This exquisite weight is faceted and limited to 1000 pieces. $195.

ANTIQUE PAPERWEIGHTS

ANTIQUE WEIGHTS

The classic period of paperweight manufacture is generally considered to have extended from 1840 to 1860. The idea of paperweights as a salable art form is thought to have been introduced in 1845 at the Austrian Industrial Fair in Vienna, where Pietro Bigaglia of Venice, one of a long line of Muranese glassworkers, displayed his wares. Although some weights may have been manufactured previously in France, it is believed that Bigaglia's weights may have stimulated the development of sophisticated paperweight manufacture in France.

During the classic period, three outstanding French factories set the pace in the production of paperweights: Saint Louis, Baccarat, and Clichy. Also prominent in the nineteenth century were the English factories of Bacchus and Whitefriars.

Between 1870 and 1880, the art of paperweight making migrated to the United States and continued to flourish until shortly after the turn of the century. Significant American companies were the New England Glass Company, the Boston and Sandwich Glass Co., Gillinder, Mt. Washington, and later, Millville.

Antique paperweights, especially those created in the classic period, are some of the most desirable and sought-after pieces on today's market. They represent a wide range of styles, designs, and techniques, and many are unequaled in terms of glass artistry and craftsmanship. In addition, antique weights provide a legacy of quality and beauty for contemporary glass artists and collectors.

148. ANTIQUE AMERICAN

In this classic miniature nosegay set on a crystal clear ground, three New England canes imitate tiny flowers set on a stem surrounded by green leaves. $475.

149. ANTIQUE AMERICAN

A garland of millefiori canes set on a latticinio cushion forms an intriguing composition centered around a handsome geometric cane. $350.

150. ANTIQUE AMERICAN

A lovely red poinsettia and bud, set on a fine white latticinio cushion, are augmented by allover faceting in this Sandwich Glass Company weight. $750.

151. ANTIQUE AMERICAN

Bits and pieces of complex canes and lacy twists create an intriguing arrangement in this scrambled or "end-of-day" weight from the Sandwich Glass Company. $100.

152. ANTIQUE AMERICAN

Spokes of patterned millefiori radiate from a ring of seven yellow rabbit silhouette canes. A white rabbit center cane completes the motif, which is set on a latticinio ground and highlighted by quatrefoil faceting. $675.

153. ANTIQUE AMERICAN

Two deep blue upper petals and three pink and white striped lower petals surround a millefiori center cane in this gaily colored pansy weight. Green foliage completes this Sandwich Glass Company design set in clear crystal. $600.

154. ANTIQUE AMERICAN

This striking red and white version of a marbrie weight rests on a footed pedestal base known as a piedouche. $225.

155. ANTIQUE AMERICAN

Delicately shaded from yellow to a rich, sun-ripened orange-brown, this lovely blown apple by New England Glass Company rests on a simple, clear glass "cookie" base. $550.

156. ANTIQUE AMERICAN

This unusual New England Glass Company weight features a white latticinio cushion studded with a large blue and white geometric millefiori cane. $200.

157. ANTIQUE AMERICAN

A ring of multicolored lampwork flowers encircles a brilliant red clematis in this magnum-size antique American weight. The arrangement is set in clear crystal. $375.

158. ANTIQUE AMERICAN

A charming pastel nosegay, arranged on a ground of clear crystal, is encircled by a delicate border of finely crafted millefiori canes. $625.

159. ANTIQUE AMERICAN

Four ripe pears are arranged symmetrically around a fifth in this well-formed fruit-in-a-basket weight by the Sandwich glassworks. Red cherries and emerald green leaves complete the composition. $700.

160. ANTIQUE AMERICAN

This outstanding Sandwich Glass Company weight features an arrangement of pastel millefiori canes set on a fine white latticinio cushion, enhanced by fancy faceting. $650.

161. ANTIQUE BACCARAT

This exquisite close packed millefiori weight features an assortment of charming Gridel animal silhouette canes including a stag, horse, monkey, elephant, goat, dog, and several green shamrocks. Signed and dated "B1848" in a cane within the design. $1750.

162. ANTIQUE BACCARAT

This exciting and unusual faceted "end-of-day" weight contains a piece of yellow buttercup near the center, the first bit of flower we have seen with scrambled millefiori. $650.

163. ANTIQUE BACCARAT

Five concentric rings of red, white, and blue millefiori canes are enhanced by several "arrowhead" canes, which add a touch of green to the overall color scheme. Set on a clear crystal ground. $400.

164. ANTIQUE BACCARAT

A favorite motif of Baccarat, this classic pansy with two purple velvet-like upper petals, three yellow veined lower petals, and a millefiori center, is set on a green leafy stem and encased in clear crystal. $750.

165. ANTIQUE BACCARAT

A magnificent blue and white torsade makes up the base of this close packed millefiori mushroom weight by Baccarat. $1600.

166. ANTIQUE BACCARAT

Close concentric millefiori canes in fresh delicate colors make up this miniature weight set in clear crystal. $350.

167. ANTIQUE BACCARAT

An excellent assortment of Gridel animal canes, including a rooster, horse, dog, goat, red dancing devil, hunter, and squirrel is combined with scattered millefiori on lace. Dated and signed "B1847" near the dancing devil. $1950.

168. ANTIQUE BACCARAT

Resembling a faceted jewel, this interlaced trefoil garland with Gridel animal silhouette canes is highlighted by a distinctive blue and white double overlay. $5200.

169. ANTIQUE BACCARAT

This extremely rare and unusual Baccarat weight features three exquisite red gentian flowers and one bud set on a sparkling ground of clear crystal. $6250.

170. ANTIQUE BACCARAT

A lovely blue and white primrose with a honeycomb millefiori center is encircled by a garland of well-crafted canes. The weight is faceted and has a clear, star cut base. $2000.

171. ANTIQUE BACCARAT

Set in clear, sparkling crystal, a rare amethyst-colored clematis with a white stardust center is complemented by numerous green leaves. $1850.

172. ANTIQUE BACCARAT

An attractive primrose with six white petals edged in bright red and a lovely millefiori center floats in clear crystal and is enhanced by a star cut base. $850.

173. ANTIQUE BACCARAT

Identical clematis buds entwined about a central stalk form a colorful and unusual motif set in sparkling clear crystal over a star cut base. $2000.

174. ANTIQUE BACCARAT

Vivid blue and white petals form this spectacular primrose set in sparkling crystal with eleven green leaves. $1200.

175. ANTIQUE BACCARAT

This piedouche, or footed weight, features delicate close concentric rings of Baccarat millefiori canes centered on a complex arrowhead floret. A stunning pink and white torsade rings the base. $2100.

176. ANTIQUE BACCARAT

Millefiori canes and three Gridel animal silhouette canes, a rooster, a stork, and two white lovebirds make up this miniature scattered on lace weight. $650.

177. ANTIQUE BACCARAT

Entitled "Bouquet de Marriage," this very special Baccarat mushroom weight features a carpet of white star canes with pink whorl centers surrounding an arrowhead cane. A blue spiral torsade encircles the mushroom at the base. $3500.

178. ANTIQUE BACCARAT

A *quatrefoil design made up of millefiori canes sparkles in clear crystal. A number of stunning arrowhead canes are present in the design.* $650.

179. ANTIQUE BACCARAT

This fine close concentric millefiori mushroom is centered on a shamrock cane and encircled by a spiraling blue and white torsade. $2600.

180. ANTIQUE BACCARAT

A pleasing array of lacy latticinio bits makes up this delightful scrambled or "end-of-day" weight by Baccarat. $325.

181. ANTIQUE BACCARAT

In this rare and realistic looking Baccarat weight, three finely crafted strawberries in various stages of ripeness are featured with delicate green leaves. The design is set on a clear crystal ground. $4500.

182. ANTIQUE BACCARAT

Composed of tiny mica flecks and small bits of green colored glass, this abstract "rock weight," a style unique to Baccarat, suggests the bottom of the sea or the surface of the moon. $300.

183. ANTIQUE CLICHY

A border of red and green millefiori canes surrounds a ring of eight delicate stardust canes with pink whorl centers in this miniature weight. A lavender and white cane forms the center of this distinctively lovely composition set on a crystal clear ground. $375.

184. ANTIQUE CLICHY

A collection of some of Clichy's finest millefiori canes, including green and pink roses and edelweiss canes, makes up this interlaced trefoil garland weight set on a clear ground. $1400.

185. ANTIQUE CLICHY

Sparkling complex millefiori canes centered around a well-formed pink and green Clichy rose make up this radiant concentric weight set in clear crystal. $750.

186. ANTIQUE CLICHY

In this miniature weight, a delightful millefiori nosegay, which includes a delicate pink-and-white Clichy rose, is set on a ground of sparkling clear crystal. $650.

187. ANTIQUE CLICHY

This superb example of a Clichy swirl features pristine blue-and-white spokes radiating from a pink and white Clichy rose cane. $3500.

188. ANTIQUE CLICHY

Two concentric stars made up of garlands of millefiori canes are centered around a large pastry mold cane. The motif is strikingly displayed against a brilliant turquoise color ground. $1800.

189. ANTIQUE CLICHY

A classic pink and green Clichy rose forms the center of this miniature turquoise and white swirl weight. $2650.

190. ANTIQUE CLICHY

A *bright turquoise color ground attractively displays a selection of Clichy pastry mold canes.* $1100.

191. ANTIQUE CLICHY

A *vivid turquoise and white swirl emanates from a large and brilliant center cane in this stunning Clichy weight.* $1500.

192. ANTIQUE CLICHY

Vivid Clichy colors are displayed in a myriad of large complex canes forming an exquisite close pack millefiori motif. $950.

193. ANTIQUE CLICHY

Rich colors and delicately formed canes are featured in this classic example of a patterned millefiori design, centered on a pink-and-green Clichy rose. $750.

194. ANTIQUE CLICHY

Set on a rare green "moss" ground, this very special weight features an assortment of complex millefiori canes, including three different Clichy roses. $6250.

195. ANTIQUE CLICHY

A "sodden snow" ground sets off crisp and colorful millefiori canes arranged in an exquisite star pattern. $750.

196. ANTIQUE CLICHY

In this elegant chequer weight, white latticinio twists divide a variety of intensely colored millefiori canes centered around a classic Clichy rose. $1500.

197. ANTIQUE CLICHY

A variety of millefiori canes form five circlets, each centered on a larger cane, including a pink and green Clichy rose. This fascinating design is enhanced by allover side faceting and set on a crystal clear ground. $1500

198. ANTIQUE CLICHY

Dozens of tiny white stars make up a central millefiori cane surrounded by patterned millefiori on a rich translucent blue ground. $1100.

199. ANTIQUE CLICHY

This is an excellent example of a Clichy "end-of-day" weight, characteristically the most colorful of all scrambled paperweights. This fine piece contains bits of pink and green as well as pink and white Clichy roses. $325.

200. ANTIQUE CLICHY

A bright and interesting array of Clichy canes is divided by lacy twists of latticinio in this stunning chequer weight. $900.

201. ANTIQUE SAINT LOUIS

An exquisite millefiori nosegay set in clear crystal on a "strawberry cut" base is enhanced by complex faceting. $750.

202. ANTIQUE SAINT LOUIS

A swirling white latticinio bed is the backdrop for patterned millefiori edged by a stunning ring of pink and green millefiori canes. $600.

203. ANTIQUE SAINT LOUIS

A rare motif in antique Saint Louis weights, a single ripe pear hanging from a leafy branch is elegantly set on a star cut base. $2750.

204. ANTIQUE SAINT LOUIS

A large cane featuring the silhouette of a dog forms the center of this jasper panel weight. Eight additional canes and opaque white stripes complete the unusual design. $1200.

205. ANTIQUE SAINT LOUIS

A *favorite flower of the classic French factories*, this lovely purple and yellow pansy by Saint Louis is set on a clear, star cut base. $450.

206. ANTIQUE SAINT LOUIS

A *stunning deep pink dahlia with a millefiori center* is accented by five emerald green leaves and set on a star cut clear base. $2650.

207. ANTIQUE SAINT LOUIS

A *perfectly formed strawberry blossom and two berries*, one ripe and the other not, rest on a beautiful swirling white latticinio cushion. $3250.

208. ANTIQUE SAINT LOUIS

Fresh pears, cherries, and a ripe yellow apple make up this superb Saint Louis fruit assemblage centered on a white latticinio cushion. $1400.

209. ANTIQUE SAINT LOUIS

A simple arrangement of two cherries on a leafy branch appears as a complex, brightly colored cluster in this highly faceted weight set in clear crystal. $2500.

210. ANTIQUE SAINT LOUIS

This fine example of a pink camomile or pompon with matching bud and four green leaves is set on a beautiful white latticinio ground. $2000.

211. ANTIQUE SAINT LOUIS

In this unusual miniature weight, a white latticinio cushion set on a rare tomato-red ground forms a striking backdrop for a pristine white camomile and bud. $2200.

212. ANTIQUE SAINT LOUIS

A blue and white spiral torsade forms a spectacular backdrop for a well-formed upright bouquet made up of a pure white clematis, three smaller flowers, and a number of handsome green leaves. $2200.

213. ANTIQUE SAINT LOUIS

A graceful fuchsia blossom and buds are set against a perfectly formed latticinio cushion in this realistic and elegant Saint Louis weight. $2850.

214. ANTIQUE SAINT LOUIS

A delicate red, white, and blue upright bouquet with rich green foliage is enhanced by a blue spiral torsade, which appears multiplied by allover faceting. $2800.

215. ANTIQUE SAINT LOUIS

A vivid blue double clematis is surrounded by deep green leaves, and centered around a distinctive serrated cane. Set on a cushion of white latticinio threads, the weight is beautifully faceted. $1200.

216. ANTIQUE SAINT LOUIS

Unusual veined petals centered on a millefiori cane and complemented by bright green leaves form this elegant Saint Louis motif. Set in clear crystal, the design is featured on a star cut base. $1900.

217. ANTIQUE SAINT LOUIS

A truly beautiful miniature weight, this brilliant gem by Saint Louis features exquisitely formed and regally colored millefiori canes in a close concentric pattern. $1350.

218. ANTIQUE SAINT LOUIS

In this classic nosegay weight, four Saint Louis millefiori canes imitate tiny flowers set on delicate green leaves. The design, which floats in clear crystal, is surrounded by a garland of colorful millefiori canes. $650.

219. ANTIQUE SAINT LOUIS

A scrambled array of bright colors and bits of lovely latticinio canes make up this delightful "end-of-day" weight by Saint Louis. $250.

220. ANTIQUE SAINT LOUIS

Brilliant canes set in a concentric pattern form the tuft of this unusual millefiori mushroom encircled by a rare salmon-colored torsade and set on a star cut base. $3500.

221. ANTIQUE SAINT LOUIS

Pale lavender and white top petals complement three deep yellow and purple bottom petals in this charming Saint Louis pansy set on a clear, star cut base. $1900.

222. ANTIQUE SAINT LOUIS

Set on a rich red and white jasper ground, five delicate millefiori canes with arrow cane centers surround a large central complex cane. $400.

223. ANTIQUE WHITEFRIARS

In this appealing and characteristic Whitefriars design, well-spaced concentric circles of millefiori canes are set on a sparkling clear ground. $300.

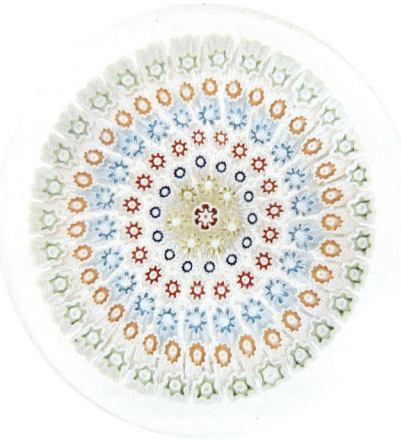

224. ANTIQUE WHITEFRIARS

Six concentric circles of pastel millefiori canes are featured in this magnum-sized weight by Whitefriars of England. $450.

225. ANTIQUE BACCHUS

An array of millefiori canes and clusters is separated by latticinio twists in this striking garnet-colored chequer design edged with a ring of clear crystal $550.

226. PANTIN

This rare and elegant Pantin weight features a golden pear suspended from a leafy branch set in sparkling crystal. $3750.

227. ANTIQUE BOHEMIAN

Richly colored patterned millefiori canes are set off by a ground of white lace in this well-designed Bohemian weight. $375.

228. ANTIQUE VAL ST. LAMBERT

Bright colors and intricate canes make up this unusual spaced concentric millefiori weight. Set on a cushion of parallel lacy twists, the motif is encircled by red, white, and blue twist sections. $550.

PAPERWEIGHT RELATED OBJECTS

229. PERTHSHIRE

Concentric millefiori set on a translucent color ground (colors vary) form the base of this perfume bottle. It is signed in the center of the base with a "P" cane. Approximately 5½" tall. $95.

230. PERTHSHIRE

A gentian blue flower with an exquisite millefiori cane center is set on a bed of upset muslin in this distinctive ashtray by Perthshire. Approximately four inches in diameter. Colors vary. $95.

231. PERTHSHIRE

This beautifully designed scrambled millefiori bottle with stopper stands approximately five inches tall. Each piece is unique in its coloration. $60.

232. PERTHSHIRE

In the base of this exquisite Perthshire shot-glass is a lovely pink lampwork flower set on a translucent blue ground. The piece is faceted in such a way that the flower appears to ring the sides of the glass. $92.50.

233. PERTHSHIRE

Close packed millefiori form the base for this inkwell and stopper. Both are faceted and the millefiori rests on a cobalt-blue base. Approximately 6 inches tall, 3½ inches in diameter. $350.

234. MODERN SAINT LOUIS

The highlight of this superb crystal tumbler is an enamel-on-gold inclusion of the Legion of Honor Medal. $500.

235. SAINT LOUIS

This unusual display of lampwork flowers is reminiscent of the rare plaque produced in Massachusetts in the 1880s. It measures approximately 4" x 6" and is limited to 25 pieces. Bouquets vary in color. $2800.

236. SAINT LOUIS

Saint Louis created this elegant penholder featuring a red and white honeycomb motif atop a paperweight base made up of scattered millefiori canes on a lacy cushion. Signed, dated, and limited to 250 pieces. $540.

237. SAINT LOUIS

This elegant translucent green wafer dish with a white torsade rim is set on a jewel-like base of concentric millefiori canes. Approximately four inches tall, this exquisite piece is signed SL1983 in a cane. Part of a limited edition of 200 to be issued in 1983. $780.

238. VICTOR TRABUCCO

A dainty purple violet blooms in the clear base of this elegantly designed perfume bottle. Approximately six inches tall, this work is signed, numbered and limited to 75 pieces. $450.

239. ANTIQUE CLICHY BOTTLE

This magnificently shaped bottle features a concentric millefiori on turquoise base with a pink and green rose center. A close packed millefiori stopper, with a turquoise and white stave neck, rests in an attractive torsade rim. $3750.

240. ANTIQUE SAINT LOUIS

A crystal clear wafer dish rimmed with an elegant blue and white torsade rests on a scrambled millefiori base. Approximately three inches tall. $1200.

241. ANTIQUE SAINT LOUIS

Known in Victorian society as a handcooler, this brilliant egg shaped paperweight is made up of dozens of finely crafted close packed millefiori canes. $1200.

242. ANTIQUE WHITEFRIARS INKWELL

Dated 1848, this charming Whitefriars inkwell presents a close concentric millefiori base which is complemented by a matching stopper. This piece is four inches in diameter at the base and stands six inches tall. $600.

243. ANTIQUE WHITEFRIARS DOORSTOP

This unusual piece, which stands approximately four inches tall, includes five richly colored millefiori panels encased in sparkling crystal. $900.

GLOSSARY

Air Ring An elongated air inclusion encircling a weight near the base, usually above and below a torsade.

Arrow Cane A millefiori section made from rods containing a three-pronged arrow motif.

Base The bottom of a paperweight.

Basket An outer row of millefiori canes, pulled together underneath the motif to form a staved enclosure for the decorative elements; a latticinio ground pulled down in the center (as in Saint Louis and American fruit weights).

Bouquet A floral design comprising more than one flower.

Cane The small piece of a molded or bundled glass rod that has been pulled out so that an intricate pattern appears in cross section.

Carpet Ground An overall pattern of identical millefiori canes used as a backdrop for a pattern of other canes or decorative elements.

Chequer Weight A paperweight in which the millefiori canes are separated by short lengths of latticinio twists in a checkerboard fashion.

Cinquefoil A garland of canes having five loops.

Clear Ground Term used for a weight in which the motif rests on clear glass.

Close Concentric Millefiori A common spacing scheme in millefiori weights featuring tightly packed concentric circles of canes.

Close Millefiori General name for any spacing scheme in millefiori weights which features tightly packed random arrangement of canes.

Color Ground Term used when transparent or opaque colored glass has been used as the background for a paperweight motif.

Edelweiss Cane A white millefiori cane of star shape surrounding a core of bundled yellow rods—resembling the Swiss national flower.

Facet The flat or concave surface formed when the side or top (or both) of a paperweight is shaped with a flat or rounded grinding wheel.

Floret See CANE.

Garland General name for any spacing scheme in millefiori weights which features one or more chains of canes.

Hand Cooler An egg-shaped paperweight, once a common accessory for ladies.

Jasper Ground Paperweight backdrop formed by a mixture of two colors of finely ground glass.

Lace (Muslin or Upset Muslin) White or colored glass thread spiralled around a clear rod. Short lengths are used in a jumbled arrangement to form a background for the decorative elements.

Latticinio A swirl or spiral arrangement of many white or colored threads of glass used as a paperweight ground.

Magnum A paperweight with a diameter exceeding 3¼ inches.

Millefiori From the Italian phrase for "a thousand flowers." Used to describe the composite glass cross-section used in many paperweights.

Miniature A paperweight with a diameter of less than 2 inches.

Muslin See LACE.

Nosegay A motif consisting of a flat bouquet using millefiori canes as flowers.

Overlay Weight A paperweight that has been coated with one (single overlay), two (double overlay), or three (triple overlay) layers of glass and then had windows or facets cut in it to allow visual access to the inner motif. Flash overlays are coated with translucent glass before cutting.

Piedouche French term for footed weight.

Pinchbeck Weight Metallic disk made of a zinc-copper alloy and featuring a design in bas-relief. The disk is covered with a magnifying lens which is then fitted to a pewter or alabaster base.

Quatrefoil A four-lobed design used as a garland pattern; a faceting scheme.

Rod A cylindrical length of glass, most often containing a simple molded design of more than one color; the basic component of a millefiori cane.

Scrambled Millefiori A millefiori paperweight design in which whole and broken canes, and sometimes white or colored lace are jumbled together to fill the weight.

Signature Cane A millefiori cane bearing the name or initials of the weight's factory of origin or artist who created it.

Silhouette Cane A millefiori cane which in cross section reveals the silhouette of an animal, flower, or human figure.

Star Cut A many-pointed star incised into the base of a weight for decoration.

Sulphide A three-dimensional ceramic medallion or portrait plaque used as a decorative enclosure for a paperweight or other glass object.

Torsade An opaque glass thread loosely wound around a filigree core, usually found near the base of a mushroom weight.

Trefoil A garland with three loops.

Upright Bouquet A three-dimensional grouping of canes and stylized lampwork flowers set on a bed of leaves.

SULPHIDES

ABOUT SULPHIDES

A BRIEF HISTORY OF SULPHIDES

Sometimes, amidst the many colorful millefiori and lampwork paperweights, we tend to overlook the simple elegance and artistic beauty of the oldest and one of the most fascinating of all paperweight styles—the sulphide.

Sulphides are sculpted ceramic cameos encased in crystal. The technique, which was first developed during the 1750s in France, was often used to commemorate historical events and famous personalities. This combination of history and art intrigued collectors from the start and even the earliest pieces sold for formidable prices.

Throughout the 19th century, hundreds of sulphides were created to ornament a variety of glass articles including decanters, perfumes, seals, candlesticks, buttons, jewelry, and paperweights. These early glass incrustations were highly regarded works of art and many were considered important historical documents as well. Napoleon placed three sulphides bearing his image in the cornerstone of the famous "Cour de Comptes." In another instance, a lead box with "several crystal portraits" of Louis XIV was placed in the foundation stone of a monument to the monarch.

Towards the turn of the century, the popularity of sulphides declined and for nearly 80 years no work was done in the field. It wasn't until the 1950s that glass artists attempted to rediscover the almost forgotten technique of sulphide production. Test after test was conducted and finally, after numerous failures, an antique sulphide was shattered in order to analyze the composition of the cameo and reconstruct the formula.

Since the revival of the sulphide technique, this unique art form has attracted a number of prominent sculptors and glass artists. Albert David and Robert Cochet, both official sculptors for the French Mint, are well known for their sulphide work. Dora Maar, a protegee of Picasso, crafted an outstanding cameo of Winston Churchill.

The most well known and prolific sulphide artist is Gilbert Poillerat, a French sculptor and professional medal engraver. He has created exceptional pieces for the famous glass factories of Saint Louis, Baccarat, and Cristalleries d'Albret. One of his works, Eustace Tilley, the mythical high-hatted, monocled character who appears in *The New Yorker* magazine, is considered one of the rarest of all contemporary sulphides. Produced by Baccarat in commemoration of the magazine's 30th anniversary, only six weights were issued—four regular editions and two overlays. Today these pieces are considered some of the most unique and valuable of all modern sulphides.

Another exceptional Baccarat sulphide is Poillerat's "George Washington" commemorative done in 1954. The example pictured below is enhanced by a diamond-cut ground and a richly colored double overlay. A great deal of variety in both cutting and ground color is found in these early sulphides.

Each sulphide provides a window to history and offers a unique way to pass this history from generation to generation. These small and precious works of art play an integral part in the development of paperweights and are extremely important pieces for every collection. Many of the sulphides in this brochure are being offered at issue price and represent excellent investments for collectors. L.H. Selman Ltd. will be happy to advise you in selecting those sulphides which will most complement your collection.

EUSTACE TILLEY, *one of the rarest and most valuable modern Baccarat sulphides. Regular, limited to 4.*

GEORGE WASHINGTON, *sculpted by Gilbert Poillerat. Regular, limited to 1182. Overlay limited to 200.*

SULPHIDES HISTORY 117

HOW SULPHIDES ARE MADE

The creation of a sulphide is a technically complex and painstaking process. First, the artist prepares numerous drawings and detailed plans. From these, a model five times larger than the cameo is made from plastic molding clay. At this stage, special attention must be paid to the details of the sculpture to allow for the eventual five to one reduction of the design. The model is cast in plaster, the surface refined, and minute changes are made. From this piece the caster makes a bronze portrait which is polished and mounted on a reduction lathe where a faithful reproduction one fifth smaller than the bronze image is cut into steel.

A carefully prepared mixture of clay, sand, and soapstone is poured into a plaster cast made from the steel mold. The cameo is hydraulically pressed and heat treated, place on a circular steel plate, then gently covered with a gather of molten crystal. Another mass of clear or colored glass is added to form the ground of the weight.

The paperweight is annealed and the bottom carefully ground and polished. The refraction of light playing through the glass gives a brilliant appearance to the encased cameo.

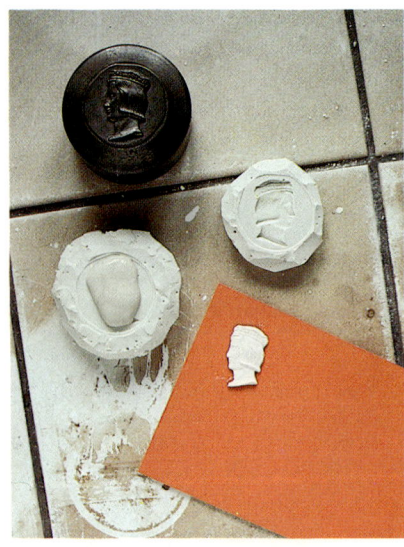

A sulphide cameo is produced from a plaster cast which has been formed in a steel mold.

A paste of clay, sand, and soapstone is poured into a plaster cast.

PAPERWEIGHT • PRESS
SANTA CRUZ • CALIFORNIA